T0062896

Nowhere to Run

Nowhere to Run

A Surgeon's Tale from the Gaza Strip

Suheal A. Khan

PARTRIDGE

Print information available on the last page.

To order additional copies of this book, contact
Toll Free 800 101 2657 (Singapore)
Toll Free 1 800 81 7340 (Malaysia)
orders.singapore@partridgepublishing.com

www.partridgepublishing.com/singapore

Contents

To my parents and my wife, Penpichaya.

Preface

Sitting down to write my experiences in Gaza was a sad exercise. As I wrote this book, the Gaza Strip was being attacked again by the Israeli Defence Force (IDF) in July 2014.

It was truly a pleasure and an insight working in the Gaza Strip, and I left many friends behind to face oppression there. For this I feel guilty, and I truly wish for an end to this senseless conflict.

The Gazan predicament will continue for a few more generations. I do not see an end to this stalemate, and we will unfortunately see more innocent victims of the atrocious, indiscriminate bombings carried out by the IDF and more provocation from Hamas by firing rockets into Israel.

The world has to wake up and see the apartheid being imposed on the Palestinians by the occupying might and force of Israel. One cannot continue to look away from this injustice and from the plight of the Gazans.

The Israeli government has been quick to blame Gaza's troubles on Hamas, as if Israel had no responsibility for what has happened in this narrow, overpopulated stretch of land. That, too, is a conviction that lacks context.

Ariel Sharon pulled the Israeli military and settlers out of Gaza in 2005, but according to the United Nations, Israel continues to control Gaza's coastline and airspace and remains an occupying power. Israel, along with the United States, has helped create a political and humanitarian nightmare in Gaza.

During the wars over Gaza, Hamas has displayed a willingness to kill many of Gaza's citizens, including women and children, in order to embarrass the Israelis internationally. Hamas's rockets are not really weapons of war but of terror and propaganda. They provoke the Israelis into brutal reprisals that Hamas hopes will discredit Israel's reputation abroad and portray Hamas among Muslims, Palestinians, and Arab states as brave freedom fighters. Gaza's citizens become unwitting hostages in this struggle. In spite of this, Hamas retains support in Gaza and has become increasingly popular in the West Bank, which testifies to the intense anger that Palestinians feel toward continued Israeli rule and the blockade.

Many of the characters in this book are real and most alive today, but their names have been changed to protect their identities. I have told my experiences in Gaza, warts and all, and I hope this book does not offend anyone. It's not meant to incite anger; it is just the truth, as I saw it.

My thoughts are with the oppressed, beautiful, friendly, and welcoming people of the Gaza Strip. May your God be with you.

All the monies raised from the sale of this book will help fund the Mobile International Surgical Teams Foundation in its humanitarian and educational projects around the world (www.mistngo.co.uk).

June 2016

1

Waiting

The Gaza Strip is a piece of land thirty-six kilometres long and ten kilometres miles wide (365 kilometres square) that houses 1.5 million Palestinians, half of whom are under the age of twelve. To the west lies the Mediterranean Sea; to the south, Egypt and the border crossing at Rafah. In the east and north lies Israel, with its border crossing in the north at Erez. Off the coast lies the Israeli navy, and it does not allow fishermen to venture more than one kilometre from the Gazan coast. Essentially, the Gaza Strip has become the world's largest prison. Access into the Gaza Strip is only allowed by the Israelis and Egyptians, through the border crossings and port (Figure 1).

Our medical team consisted of

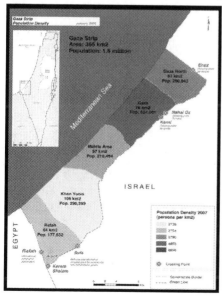

Map of the Gaza Strip

1

three: an anaesthetist, an operating-department practitioner (ODP), and me, a trauma surgeon with expertise in limb reconstruction using external fixation devices. We all belonged to the MiST Foundation (Mobile International Surgical Teams, www.mistngo.co.uk), a surgical aid agency based in the United Kingdom. We had arrived six weeks after the initial attack on the Gaza Strip in December 2008 by the Israeli army, known as the Israeli Defence Force (IDF). We had brought enough medical equipment to treat twenty patients, but we were trapped and frustrated, awaiting our time to enter the Gaza Strip in an Egyptian town, Al Arish, ten miles from the Gazan border.

One could see the Gaza Strip in the distance across the bay, as the Mediterranean coast swung round north. Sitting on the beach in Al Arish in Egypt, one could hear the bombs dropping in the distance with a resonance and impact that made the ground shudder. The plumes of smoke rising in the distance served as a constant reminder that only a short distance away, the Gazans were being bombed, and lives were being lost. The many injured awaited medical help. The Gaza Strip was surrounded on all sides; the Palestinians had nowhere to run and hide from the IDF bombing onslaught.

Our first team, Egyptian MiST, had already been to Gaza within the first few weeks of the war and had set up initial links with the Gazan medics. The team had worked out of Nasser Hospital in Khan Yunis in the southern part of the strip.

We reached Rafah in the minibus we hired in Cairo, spending eight hours travelling across the Sinai Desert to the border crossing from Egypt into Gaza. Surprisingly, it was cold and windy, not the weather we were expecting in January in this part of the world (Figure 2).

**Author (on right) arriving at Egyptian/
Gaza border crossing at Rafah**

On our arrival at the Rafah border crossing, we were turned away by the Egyptian guards, who said we did not have permission to enter. There were at least fifty other people waiting to cross the border from other aid agencies; some had been waiting for a month. As there were no facilities at the border save a small coffee shop, we decided to head to the nearest town, Al Arish in Egypt. There we hoped to book into rooms at a hotel and wait for our access into Gaza.

Permission to enter the Gaza Strip had to be sought, somewhat ironically, from the Israelis, who had started the bombing on Gaza. As a specialist humanitarian organisation, the MiST Foundation was trying all its diplomatic and medical contacts to get access into the strip.

At ten o'clock each morning, Peter, our ODP, would head down to the Gazan border at Rafah and ask the Egyptian guards whether our names had been listed as aid workers allowed to enter. After a time, it became a bit of a joke, one Peter described as Monty Pythonesque:

Peter: 'Can I go into Gaza?'

Guard: 'No, but you can have a cup of tea.'

The Egyptian guards were always polite to Peter. They invited him into their office but gave nothing away. Peter often met other aid workers in the same predicament. As we shared a humanitarian background and this common experience at the border, I befriended a great many of them. I am still in touch with many of them today (Figure 3).

Peter (in centre) befriending other aid workers at the Egyptian Rafah border.

To while away our time at Al Arish, we played football on the beach, read, and prepared ourselves mentally for the challenges ahead. Peter and I had experience in treating patients in difficult situations such as after natural disasters, when facilities and equipment are sparse, but this was our first time travelling to a war zone.

The delegation from another humanitarian organisation, a group of Palestinian doctors practicing in England (many of whom were originally from the Gaza Strip), was staying in the same hotel at Al Arish. As we sat in the bar, getting to know one another, we were constantly being monitored by the Egyptian secret police, the Machaborat.

It was 11 p.m. on our fourth day of waiting in Al Arish when Ahmed, a Palestinian physician from England, came to my room and told me that there was someone he would like me to meet. I went across to his room, and there, sitting on the floor, was an Arab, a Bedouin. For $1,000, this Bedouin would get us all into Gaza either via the tunnels or through a break in the fence the Bedouin knew about. I was apprehensive. I knew the Palestinian doctors were desperate to get into Gaza; some still had family there. Could we trust the Bedouin? He might lead us into a trap with the IDF waiting for us. My sixth sense kicked in. I thanked the man for his offer of help and told him we would wait for a diplomatic solution to enter Gaza. I had been in contact with the British Embassy in Cairo as well as the Foreign and Commonwealth Office in London to lobby for our and the UK Palestinian doctors' entry into the Gaza Strip.

On the sixth day, we had word from the British Embassy in Cairo. The MiST Foundation had been given permission to enter Gaza, but through the Israeli-controlled Erez border crossing in the north of the Gaza Strip. This prospect was impossible for us; it would mean travelling all the way back to Cairo and then flying to Tel Aviv to get to the border crossing with all our medical equipment. Once we arrived at Erez, there was no guarantee we would actually be allowed to enter Gaza.

I implored the envoy at the British Embassy to realise this proposal by the Israelis was impossible, as we had only a finite time away from our places of work in the United Kingdom. Instead, he must persuade the Egyptians to let us enter through the Rafah border crossing with our UK Palestinian colleagues, who were all British citizens and doctors. It soon became clear that the Egyptians did what the Israelis wanted. By proxy, the Israelis also controlled the Egyptian Rafah border!

At 8 p.m. on the eighth day in Al Arish, the word came through: entry to Gaza was allowed for us all, but we needed to get to the border within the next hour, before the crossing closed for the night.

With a combination of elation and blind panic, we packed the minibuses with the medical kit and personnel and headed for Rafah at top speed. We were met by a bunch of indignant Egyptian guards. In fact, the guards were downright rude and bullied us into the immigration hall. This confrontational attitude was uncalled for. After all, we were going to Gaza to help, and we had nothing to do with any terrorist organisations. The Egyptian guards demanded that we open all the boxes. I told the guards to use the X-ray machines to scan the boxes, as it was all medical equipment for humanitarian purposes and there was no need to open the boxes and cause more delays and hassle (Figure 4).

Taking our medical kit across Rafah border from Egypt

Finally, after an administrative process of about one hour, we were allowed to enter Gaza. We were then shepherded into a bus that would ferry us across the two-hundred-metre expanse of no-man's land into the Gaza Strip.

We had finally arrived in Gaza. Our reception at the arrivals hall in Gaza was that of heroes entering a war zone (Figure 5).

**Welcome by Hamas into the Gaza Strip
after our long wait in Al Arish, Egypt.**

The Gazans were very appreciative of our arrival, and after the formalities of getting our passports stamped, we travelled into Gaza City in a convoy of trucks along the only main road from north to south.

A hotel had been arranged for us on the seafront in Gaza City. The Adam Hotel would become my home for the next two weeks (and on future visits to Gaza). As it was midnight, and we were travelling in the dark, we could not make out the destruction inflicted on Gaza.

The following day, officials from the Ministry of Health and the dean of the medical school, himself a general surgeon, came to the hotel to welcome us formally. We were to go on a tour of Gaza and then head to the hospitals that were waiting for our help and input.

2
The Tour

The tour of the Gaza Strip was eye opening; the destruction was clearly visible (Figure 7).

Destruction of a government building in Gaza City

The stories they the Gazans told were shocking. The IDF had attacked Gaza from all sides: shelling from the sea by the navy; bombing so-called strategic targets from the air; and incursions by the IDF infantry (Figure 8).

Destroyed dock area of Gaza City

On the morning of the attack in December 2008, the IDF's targets were clearly military in nature, but many civilians were also caught up in the bombing raids. The only docks in Gaza – the fire-service headquarters and the police training school – were shelled. At the police centre, seventy-five recruits were massacred in the courtyard.

The Islamic University of Gaza (IUG) laboratories, medical school, and outbuildings were bombed. Schools, hospitals, and emergency vehicles became targets. The IDF stated that these buildings were being used by Hamas fighters behind a human shield. The laboratories at the university were making bombs, according to the IDF, so they constituted a legitimate target (Figures 9a and 9b)

IUG before bombing by IDF

Following bombing of IUG

During the war, Hamas fighters (Al Qassam Brigade) captured some Israeli soldiers. Having learned from their previous experience, the IDF no longer 'chipped' their soldiers' clothes with an electronic tag but put a chip under the skin of each soldier so they could be tracked. The IDF did not want another kidnapping of soldiers as hostages, as in the case of Corporal Gilad Shalit. The latter had been kidnapped from an IDF checkpoint after the Gazans had tunnelled under the area.

After capturing the Corporal, he was stripped of his clothes that had been 'chipped' by the IDF and scurried back along the tunnel into Hamas controlled Gaza, where he was held captive until a prisoner exchanged was arranged at a later date.

Instead of sending in troops to rescue these captured soldiers, the IDF bombed the buildings where the signal from the *chips* was emanating from, killing both their own soldiers and their captors. There was no way the IDF would leave any troops in the hands of Hamas; they thought it better to kill their own than to risk lengthy ransom deals in the future.

As we toured the Gaza Strip in our minibuses guarded by Hamas officials, it soon became clear nothing was sacred in this recent war. The IDF had sent in tanks desecrating graveyards and attacking mosques. Anything that moved was deemed an enemy. All the civilians in Gaza were legitimate targets (Figure 10).

Desecration of Gazan cemetery by the IDF

To be ruled by a democratically elected group was not acceptable to the West, who had labelled Hamas as a terrorist organization. If a population can elect terrorists as their leaders then all the population must also be terrorists, it seems.

Fifteen hundred Gazans had been killed in the first few weeks of the war, and many more lay injured and dying. With a population of 1.5 million, with over half less than 12 years old, it was inevitable that children would be also be killed and injured (Figure 11).

View of the destruction of the central area after bombing of Gaza by the IDF

On our tour, we saw makeshift refugee camps set up by international aid agencies. Some of the refugees were once more living in tents in bare-bones conditions (Figures 12, 13, and 14).

Makeshift refugee camp for those with no homes
after the bombing of the Gaza Strip

Refugee tent provided by UNICEF

**View inside a tent showing
a displaced family**

However, surprisingly, spirits were high. Everywhere I visited, children ran up greeting us (Figures 15 and 16).

**Children of the makeshift refugee camp
with the author**

Evening view of a bombed area of Gaza

Following the tour of destruction, we headed to the main hospital in Gaza City. Al Shifa Hospital was situated in the heart of Gaza City; it was a seventies-style, communist-looking grey building with approximately six hundred inpatient beds. During the IDF attack, this and many other hospitals had been inundated with causalities. How the staff had coped is a testament to the Gazan spirit. As we arrived in the car park of the hospital, an ambulance which had been struck by an Israeli rocket was on display (Figure 17).

An ambulance hit by an Israeli rocket on its way to the hospital with civilian causalities inside

The driver and all the causalities had perished under the rocket attack. Even though the ambulance had a red cross on its roof, it was still not immune from Israeli attack. The son of the director of the Al Shifa hospital had been the driver of the ambulance and had died at the scene of the attack along with his passengers.

We arrived in the board room of the hospital and were met by the director and chief medical officer. On the table was a shell that had been fired at the hospital by the IDF (Figure 18a). Many other hospitals had been attacked during the IDF onslaught as legitimate targets hiding Hamas fighters (Figure 18b).

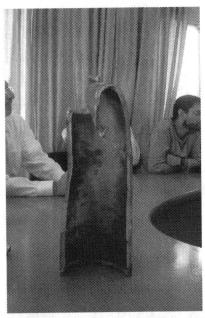

A shell found in the grounds of Al Shifa hospital in Gaza City

Red Crescent hospital bombed by IDF

After the customary tea and greetings, the director told us of the difficulties faced by the hospital during the attack, including limited medical supplies, limited experienced staff, and little equipment.

We were taken on a tour of the hospital. As in any developing country, the facilities were basic but adequate; I had worked in worse situations than this such as in Pakistan and Haiti after earthquakes had destroyed their respective regions and most facilities.

Our greeting by the orthopaedic surgeons on the wards was one of gratitude and suspicion. I could understand these men and women had been under great stress treating the injured during the bombings. Now it had been almost two months since the bombings, so what were doctors doing coming to Gaza now? Was it just morbid curiosity?

After an exchange of cigarettes and some time sipping coffee, the surgeons relaxed in my company, and the conversation started to flow. I suggested we do a ward round and see what was needed to be done. Following this ward round it was clear that the doctors had done a remarkable job in the initial phases of the war despite their lack of equipment and expertise.

Many of the surgeons were young and newly qualified, with degrees from places such as Kazakhstan, Ukraine, and other Eastern Bloc countries. Their clinical experience was limited, so with these constraints I congratulated them on a job well done. We returned to the office for some tea and cigarettes. As they relaxed even more, they started to pull out X-rays of cases that needed some input.

After any disaster there is a bimodal distribution for limb amputations. In the initial phase of a disaster, amputation may be essential to save a life. Now we were in the second phase of the bimodal distribution, where mal-unions and infections of initial open fractures may require amputations. This was my field of expertise as a limb reconstruction surgeon with experience using the Ilizarov method and external fixators (Appendix 1). In my experience, it is always better to preserve a limb rather than amputate and then rely on prosthetics for the rest of the patient's life. It is difficult trying to find your leg when you are seventy years old and going to the toilet in the middle of the night!

I gave suggestions for their clinical cases, and the Gazan surgeons were extremely grateful and asked whether I would be happy to show them the surgical techniques. I gladly agreed but wished to meet with the head of department first.

The following morning, I arrived at Al Shifa and met the head of the orthopaedic department. An amicable and well-spoken man, he turned to me and suggested we go across the road to a café and smoke a shisha. It was nine thirty in the morning! I of course agreed, and as we walked we talked.

We arrive at the café, and it could have been some place off the Seine in Paris; the setting was very cosmopolitan and tastefully furnished. The waiters were polite, and after ordering we discussed the situation in Gaza. We never returned to the hospital, just sat there most of the morning talking (Figure 19).

Sitting with head of Al Shifa orthopaedic department having coffee at a café opposite Al Shifa hospital

Prior to coming to Gaza, I had been briefed by Egyptian MiST that Al Shifa was a political nightmare to work at. There was much in-fighting, as in any orthopaedic department, and we were advised not to base our operations out of such an institution. Our goal was to work out of Nasser Hospital in Khan Yunis. Egyptian MiST had already treated patients there who needed follow-up, and the orthopaedic department and administration were very accommodating to foreign talent.

I expressed my views to the Ministry of Health MoH the following day, and they arranged for me to visit and work at Nasser Hospital for the rest of my two-week stay in Gaza. My reception at the hospital was befitting a celebrity! The previous MiST unit from Egypt had told them of my upcoming visit to Gaza, and the hospital administration had been primed. The doctors and nurses were very welcoming, and after a visit around the hospital we got down to seeing patients on a ward round and listing some of the injured who were ready for operation in the coming days.

Many of the injured had open limb fractures which had developed infections or a mal-union of the bones. This was my field of expertise, and I was very happy in the next few days, teaching and training the local staff in the art of Ilizarov surgery. We had brought $250,000 worth of kit from the United Kingdom with us, and soon we were operating in their rudimentary theatre suite.

Our first surgical case was a fourteen-year-old boy who had been playing football on an open field when an IDF helicopter gunship sprayed them with bullets (Figure 20).

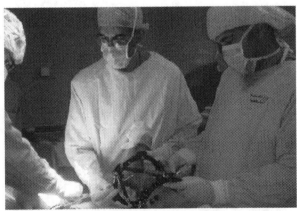

Teaching Nasser surgeon application of ring fixators (author in centre)

He suffered an open tibial fracture, which was mal-united with an open wound still present. We applied a ring fixator, addressed the wound, and had the boy standing up on crutches the next day to the amazement of his parents (Figures 21 and 22). It would take approximately three months for the fracture and soft tissue to heal, but in the meantime with the frame on his injured leg, the patient was fully weight bearing, which would stimulate the bone to heal.

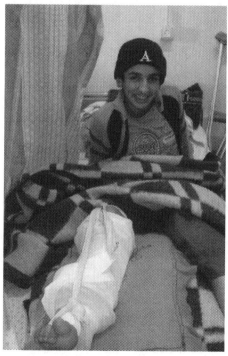

Young boy post-op ring fixator

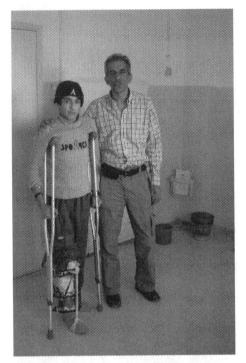

Standing with crutches the day after surgery

After spending two weeks in Gaza, I was deeply impressed at the mental strength and good humour of the Gazans. I visited the Minister of Health and told him I would be very happy to return to Gaza on a one-year sabbatical. The minister was gracious and invited me to come for a year as a visiting professor.

So, I returned to the United Kingdom with a plan of action. It was March 2009, and I would come back to Gaza as soon as I had organized a sabbatical from my hospital in Manchester.

3

The Tunnels

During my first stay in Gaza, I was approached by an aid agency based in Manchester. The group had heard of me and wanted to take my team on a tour of the tunnels at the Rafah border. I accepted on behalf of the team, and we planned to visit the tunnels the following day after finishing work at Nasser hospital.

We were picked up from the hospital and drove up to the Rafah border. We could see the Egyptian soldiers in their watchtower some two hundred metres away (Figure 23).

Gaza side of Rafah crossing showing remaining corrugated fence, behind which are displayed tools for hire

The car stopped, and we were greeted by three masked men in full view of the Egyptians. We got out of the car and were led away behind a metal screen. There lay an opening to a tunnel three metres wide and lined with bricks. Some twenty metres below, one could see the labourers carrying buckets of sand up to the surface (Figures 24 and 25).

Entrance to a brick-lined tunnel

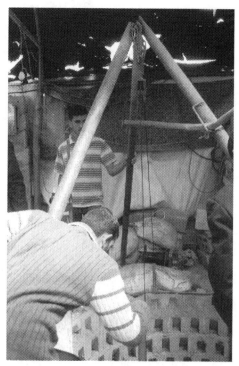

**Entrance to a tunnel at Rafah with
workers extracting soil and sand**

Amusingly, behind a metal screen shielded from the watchtowers were tools lined up used for digging: pick axes, shovels, and buckets. A sign in Arabic gave the price for hire on a daily basis. Gazans looking for work would wander down to the border, rent a shovel for a day, and help dig another tunnel (Figure 26).

**Tools on display at Rafah,
on the border with Egypt for daily hire**

The Rafah border was littered with tunnels, each one owned by a group, some of them rivals vying for the same business. The Israelis knew where the tunnels were; the Egyptians knew where the tunnels were. Everyone knew where the tunnels were, and this was big business. The tunnels would leave Gazan Rafah to wind their way across no-man's-land and open up in someone's house or shop in Egyptian Rafah.

On occasion, cars would come to the border and hook up to a pipe attached to a petrol pump in Egypt. And as if by magic, the petrol would be pumped across straight into someone's petrol tank. When petrol was scarce, the Gazans would use olive oil as fuel for their cars. They joked that after the car journey you could make falafel in the engine.

The tunnels were graded. One could drive a truck through a five-star tunnel! These tunnels were a lifeline for the besieged Gazans and also a source of money and black-market goods.

A story was told to me of an attempt to bring a sedated lion through the tunnels for the Gazan zoo. Unfortunately, the sedative wore off in the tunnel. There was great amusement and wild panic as a lion chased the workers through the tunnel. Luckily no one was injured!

Over a period of months, Gazans weakened the metal fence separating no-mans land from Gaza with blowtorches. One night in 2007, a horde of Palestinians arrived at the Rafah border, tearing down the already weakened metal fence and rushing into Egypt, overpowering the guards (Figure 27).

Border fence at Rafah cut by blow torches over a period of months before the border was stormed by Gazans

The Gazans headed to Al Arish, where they did their shopping, buying food and electrical goods before heading back into Gaza. When Hamas took control of the Gaza Strip, they started to impose taxes on goods smuggled through the tunnels; this was another source of income for an already fragile administration. The tunnels will remain until the occupation of Gaza is over and there is freedom of movement for people and goods. Until that time, there is a lot of money to be made by individual groups both in Gaza and Egypt.

4

Brief History of the Gaza Strip

Between 1917 and 1948 the Gaza Strip was part of Great Britain's Palestine mandate from the League of Nations. From the armistice agreement of 1949 until the 1967 war (with the exception of the Israeli occupation from November 1956 to March 1957), the Gaza Strip was under Egyptian administration. The 1948 Arab-Israeli war led to an influx of Palestinian Arab refugees that tripled the region's population. However, the Palestinians were never given Egyptian citizenship, remaining stateless.

After the 1967 war, Israel occupied the region and established settlements there, but autonomy for the area was promised by the 1978 Camp David accords. During the war, Israel had no idea what it would do with the territory; Levi Eshkol, Israel's prime minister at the time, called it 'a bone stuck in our throats.'

The initial settlements were established in the early 1970s. The first was Kfar Darom, which was originally established in 1946 and reformed in 1970. In 1981, as part of a peace treaty with Egypt, the last settlements of the Sinai were destroyed and some Jews moved to the Gaza Strip. Israeli settlers occupied 18 per cent of the 365-square-kilometre area. They were sparsely settled in the area as compared to the density of the Palestinian regions in the Gaza Strip.

There were twenty-one settlements in Gaza. The largest group of settlements was the Katif area, located along the southern Gaza Strip. This area contained some thirty synagogues. All of the settlements had their own schools, seminaries, stores, and doctors. These settlements blocked access to the coast from the major Palestinian cities of Khan Yunis and Rafah and cemented Israeli control of the Egypt-Gaza border.

Another group of settlements (comprising Elei Sinai, Dugit, and Nisanit) were located along Gaza's northern border with Israel, expanding the Israeli presence from the city of Ashkelon (inside Israel) to the edges of Gaza City (the Erez Industrial zone is part of this bloc). Netzarim, Kfar Darom, and Morag are strategically located in the heart of the Gaza Strip (along a north-south axis), creating a framework for Israeli control of the area and its main transportation route. These settlements divided the Gaza Strip into separate areas and isolate each area's inhabitants. In addition, the settlements control prime agricultural land, some of the area's main aquifers, and approximately one-third of the total Gaza coastline.

The Israelis had split the Gaza Strip into three sections. Between each sector the IDF had checkpoints. Normally the journey from Rafah in the south to Erez in the north, a distance of twenty-five miles, took an hour along the Omar Muktaar Road, the only main thoroughfare traversing the Gaza Strip. On occasions the IDF would stop all checkpoint crossings, trapping families in their cars in each sector. This event happened frequently, with some having to stay in their cars for days on end.

It was psychological warfare intended to undermine the freedom of the Gazans, to control them and treat them inhumanely, to break their spirits, and to kill their desires. Many Gazans told me of how they would be trapped at the whim of the IDF to open the checkpoints. Most were not allowed to leave their cars, and those who did would be under the real threat of being shot at by the IDF.

If a settler had to make a trip into Israel, the IDF would close all the checkpoints without warning so that these Israelis could make the five-mile journey across Gaza into Israel. A bridge from the settlement in the middle sector over the Omar Muktaar Road had been built for such a purpose. The Israeli settlers would be taken along this road with armed IDF protecting them on their journey out of Gaza. On their return the process was repeated.

The settlers would have to inform the IDF of when they wanted to leave Gaza, but the IDF were under no obligation to tell the Gazans the checkpoints were going to close for at least an hour until the settlers were safely across in the Holy Land.

To protect these settlers, the Israeli government was spending close to $1 million per week. The IDF also had to be aware they were targets from the Al Khassam brigade, the military arm of the political movement Hamas. Many of their soldiers had been killed, with the customary retaliation from the IDF on the local population. Hundreds were taken away for questioning following attacks on the IDF. Many would never return home but just lie incarcerated in Israeli jails.

Jews and Muslims coexisted for more than a decade, but tensions rose. In 1987, a Jewish shopper in a Gazan market was stabbed to death. The next day an Israeli truck accidentally killed four Arabs, sparking the first riots of what would become the first uprising (Intifada). With the inception of the Palestinian Intifada in Gaza, the city became a major centre of political unrest and violence. The Gaza Strip remained under frequent military curfew, imposed by Israeli troops sent to quell violence and maintain order. High unemployment and low wages have been chronic problems. As a result of the Gulf War in 1991, many Palestinian workers in that region fled back to their families in the Gaza Strip, creating a dire economic crisis and greater unemployment.

In 1993 an accord between Israel and the Palestinian Liberation Organisation (PLO) called for limited self-rule in the area. Under a May 1994 agreement, Israel's occupying forces left much of the Gaza Strip, and a Palestinian police force was deployed. Israel retained frontier areas and buffer zones around Israeli settlements. The breakdown in peace talks in 2000 and the subsequent resumption of violence hurt the local economy. Although the Gaza Strip saw less fighting with Israelis than the West Bank, in 2003 the Israeli army moved more aggressively to control sections of the Gaza Strip in response to Palestinian attacks. The Israelis also launched attacks against leaders of Hamas, which has many supporters in the territory and has carried out many suicide attacks. The Gaza Strip is also the main base for the Islamic Jihad, another militant Palestinian group. The area also was the scene of fighting between PLO-dominated Palestinian Authority forces and Hamas.

In January 2004, Israeli Prime Minister Ariel Sharon announced a plan for the withdrawal of all Israeli settlers and troops from the Gaza Strip. On August 17, 2005, Israel began to evacuate all the Jews from Gaza. The process was expected to take several weeks but took less than one. Israel and the Palestinians agreed the buildings would be razed, and the army began that process after the residents left.

A total of 1,700 families were uprooted at a cost of nearly $900 million. This included 166 Israeli farmers who produced $120 million in flowers and produce. Approximately 15 per cent of Israel's agricultural exports originated in Gaza, including 60 per cent of its cherry tomato and herb exports. Israel also lost 70 per cent of all its organic produce, which was also grown in Gaza. Since the disengagement process was completed, no Jews have been present in the Gaza Strip. Many Gazans were happy at the prospect of the IDF leaving; others were more foreboding, realizing that they were now effectively in a prison.

The Gaza Strip threatened to descend into anarchic violence after the Israeli withdrawal, with the Palestinian Authority unable to exert effective control over the territory. The Gaza Strip also continued to be a source of attacks against Israel and suffered retaliatory Israeli attacks.

In January 2006, the Palestinian Authority, at the urging of George W Bush's administration and with the grudging support of the Israelis, held elections in Gaza and the West Bank. To their surprise, Hamas won a majority of seats. The United States responded by trying to cut off aid to the Palestinian Authority, while the Israelis withheld tax revenues they had collected on the Palestinians' behalf. The United States encouraged Palestinian president Mahmoud Abbas to consolidate his power and discouraged any cooperation between Hamas and Fatah. This escalated into open warfare in June 2006, after Hamas guerrillas captured an Israeli soldier and Israel invaded the Gaza Strip, and in the following months Israel continued to mount operations into the territory.

Then, in the autumn of 2006, the Bush administration incited Fatah and its military chieftain Mohammed Dahlan (who had been angling to succeed Abbas) to attempt militarily to oust Hamas from leadership in Gaza. Fatah was defeated in the Battle of Gaza, and Hamas took charge.

The United States refused to talk to the new government, even though the United States has had relations with other governments that did not recognize Israel. Israel began its blockade of Gaza. The blockade is a base and immoral tactic that was intended to discredit Hamas by starving Gaza's citizens and wrecking Gaza's economy. The Israelis turned Gaza into a kind of wasteland.

In response to ongoing rocket attacks from the region, Israel tightened its blockade of the Gaza Strip in January 2008. The resulting shortages led Hamas to force open the Egyptian border, which had mainly been closed since 2005, for several days.

In June 2008, a six-month cease-fire was established with Israel that included a partial reopening of the border. The cease-fire largely held until a significant outbreak of fighting in November 2008 and was officially ended the next month. Late in December 2008, Israel mounted an offensive against Hamas, with ground operations in January 2009. Some 1,500 persons, about half of whom were civilians, died in the Gaza Strip before Israel and Hamas separately declared cease-fires in mid-January and Israeli forces withdrew; more than twenty thousand buildings were damaged or destroyed. Both sides subsequently were accused of war crimes by international human-rights organizations and a United Nations fact-finding mission.

In May 2010, a Turkish aid convoy challenging the blockade was boarded in international waters in a deadly raid by Israeli forces. The raid, which was widely condemned internationally, focused global attention on the blockade; Egypt subsequently reopened its border crossing, and Israel eased its blockade on imports somewhat.

By 2011, per capita income had dropped 17 per cent from 2005. Unemployment and malnutrition became rife. Israel blocked exports, including those to the West Bank. By 2011, only 3 per cent of goods exported in 2005 were being allowed out of the country. Thirty-five per cent of farmland and 85 per cent of fishing waters (a main source of food) were declared off limits by the Israelis. Gazans were denied passage to the West Bank.

Sporadic rocket and mortar attacks and Israeli air strikes, as well as minor cross-border incursions, have continued. In November 2012 Israeli air strikes, including one that killed the Hamas military chief, sparked the most intense cross-border attacks in four years.

In 1979, Israel and Egypt signed a peace treaty that returned the Sinai Peninsula, which borders the Gaza Strip, to Egyptian control. As part of that treaty, a hundred-metre-wide strip of land known as the Philadelphi Corridor was established as a buffer zone between Gaza and Egypt. Israel built a barrier there during the Palestinian uprisings of the early 2000s. The fence is made mostly of corrugated sheet metal, with stretches of concrete topped with barbed wire.

In 2005, when Israel pulled out of the Gaza Strip, Israel and Egypt reached a military agreement regarding the border, based on the principles of the 1979 peace treaty. The agreement specified that 750 Egyptian border guards would be deployed along the length of the border, and both Egypt and Israel pledged to work together to stem terrorism, arms smuggling, and other illegal cross-border activities.

From November 2005 until July 2007, the Rafah Crossing – the only entry-exit point along the Gaza-Egyptian border – was jointly controlled by Egypt and the Palestinian Authority, with the European Union monitoring Palestinian compliance on the Gaza side. After the Hamas takeover in June 2007, the European Union pulled out of the region, and Egypt agreed with Israel to shut down the Rafah Crossing, effectively sealing off the Gaza Strip on all sides. So, by proxy, Israel ultimately controls the borders and thus the entry and exit of people from the Gaza Strip.

5
Return to Gaza

Following the initial visit by Egyptian MiST and UK MiST, a further two teams from the MiST Foundation ventured to Gaza, one from Greece and another from the United Kingdom. Both teams were following up on patients already treated by the foundation and seeing new cases. In this way, the patients received continuity of care. Additionally, we were having Skype conference calls on a monthly basis with the surgeons based at Nasser hospital for updates and advice on clinical problems.

In the United Kingdom, I was working in a university teaching hospital in Manchester, running the limb reconstruction unit with my colleague. On my return from Gaza, I applied for a one-year sabbatical. By September 2009 this request had been granted, and I was all set to return to Gaza in April 2010 as a visiting professor of orthopaedics. I informed the officials in Gaza that I was to return for a year, so that I could teach and train the local surgeons in the art of Ilizarov surgery. In developing counties, it is useful to use external fixators, as they can be reused on other patients once the treatment is finished. In addition, this technique means there is no need for X-ray machines in theatre, which are expensive and invariably breakdown. Any adjustment to align the limb can be done after the operation using these external fixation devices.

In January 2010, the HR department of the hospital in Manchester asked to see me and told me that, on reflection, my request for the sabbatical had been refused. No real reason was given for their refusal. This put me in a quandary, as there were many families, surgeons, and staff members waiting for my return to Gaza.

After an appeal and re-appeal with my lawyers, I finally came to the conclusion that I had to do what was best. I resigned from my consultant post and set off for Gaza as planned in April 2010. I had no idea what I would do after my time in Gaza, but my convictions were strong. I knew I had to do this humanitarian work or regret the missed opportunity for the rest of my life.

As an optimist, I knew things would all turn out for the best. I had no regrets about leaving my comfortable job and heading to uncertainty!

6

In and Out of the Gaza Strip

The Israelis would not grant me a work permit for Gaza, so I had to leave Gaza, go back home, and re-enter two weeks later on a three-month visitor's visa. Even though I was working in the Gaza Strip, the Israelis had a say as to who would be issued with a work permit. I could go through Egypt, but that proved even more difficult than going through the Erez border controlled by the Israelis.

When entering Gaza, I would arrive at the Tel Aviv airport and immediately be picked out of the line waiting for clearance at immigration. I knew what to expect. It was usually a pretty Israeli IDF officer who interrogated me.

'Why do you have an Arabic name?'

'It's not my fault. Ask my father. He is an Arabic scholar.'

'What are you doing in Israel?'

'You know; I work for an NGO.'

'Where are you staying? What links do you have with terrorist organizations?'

'Come on, why would I tell you even if I was linked with any lunatics?'

All these questions I would answer with a smile, at the annoyance of the officer.

'Why are you so happy?'

'Because I am on my way to Gaza via Jerusalem, the holy city.'

All my papers were in order. I had clearance to enter Gaza by the WHO; the British embassy had cleared my papers and backed me to go to Gaza on humanitarian grounds. But two British Asian students had blown themselves up in Tel Aviv after collecting bombs in Gaza a few years previously, and the IDF always looked at British Asians with suspicion.

After a couple of hours of questioning and telephone calls I would be escorted to immigration, looked on by tourists standing in line. The immigration officer would stamp my passport even though I asked her not to. An Israeli stamp would not allow me into other Arabic countries in the future. She stamped the passport with a smile, knowing full well the implications of such a stamp. The guards would escort me to the luggage carousel and then to the X-ray room, where my suitcase would be examined.

All this time I would be talking to these children in IDF uniforms. Some would strike up a conversation; they were students had been told the past weekend that they would work at the airport. They were just kids studying, interested in what life was like in the United Kingdom. Many of them were pleasant and would strike up a conversation and smoke a cigarette with me.

They would escort me through customs and bid me farewell. Then I would get into the taxi which had been arranged for me for the journey to Jerusalem and the hotel in the Arabic quarter.

Yacoob, the owner of the restaurant and hotel in Jerusalem, would greet me with a hug. Arranging my transfer was his way of helping his Gazan cousins. Yacoob himself was from the West Bank (Figure 28).

**Yacoob (on left) and the author in
his Jerusalem restaurant**

Yacoob's restaurant in the heart of Jerusalem dated back to the time of the Crusaders. There was so much history and spirit in this town. I could see why so many wars had been fought to control this beautiful, historic city.

After staying overnight in Jerusalem, we would make the southern trek to Erez, an hour away by car. At Erez checkpoint, the same routine began of interrogation and waiting for hours on end. Eventually the IDF colonel would walk up to me and say my clearance was satisfactory and I could make my way to immigration (Figure 29).

**Checkpoint at Erez before being allowed
into immigration hall**

On the other side, I took about a one-kilometre walk into no-man's-land, being watched from behind by the IDF (Figures 30 and 31).

**Gazan families arriving at Erez crossing in Israel.
One must leave the car and walk towards the border
with all possessions under the watchful eyes of the IDF**

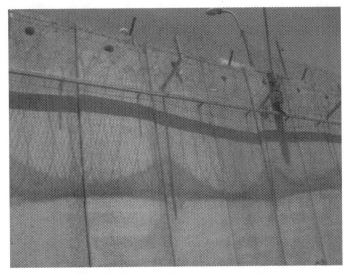

Fortified walls at the Erez crossing

Many families using this route would have to push their luggage along a covered walkway; on occasions the porters would hassle you for a tip or money just to use the walkway. I would ignore them and march onwards to my awaiting taxi, which would take me to my hotel on the seafront in Gaza City (Figure 32).

**The walk from Erez border crossing into
Gaza under a covered walkway**

On one occasion I was leaving Gaza through Erez. On the Palestinian side we had to wait for the IDF to grant us clearance to walk through no-man's-land into the Erez checkpoint.

At the Erez checkpoint, a steel door would open automatically, and we would be summoned in by Palestinian guards on the payroll of the IDF. Our bags would be scanned, and we had to remove all items into a tray for X-ray inspection. One by one we would be summoned in, over a loudspeaker, to stand in the whole-body X-ray scanner.

'Suheal, step into the scanner,' the loudspeaker would blare out. The IDF officers were watching us from a first-storey room a hundred metres away. They pronounced my Arabic name perfectly. After all, they were cousins to the Arabs, and many IDF officers were Arabs themselves living in Israel. I stepped forward into the whole-body X-ray scanner scanner

'Put your hands up and stand still, Suheal.'

I obeyed the loudspeaker, able to just make out the guards looking down on me from their first-storey lookout point behind glass windows.

On this occasion I was leaving Gaza with my friend and colleague from MiST, Peter. He was behind me and had the same routine.

'Suheal, turn right and approach the door.' I did as commanded.

'Peter, turn left and move forward.' I saw Peter obey and did not know why we were being split up. I was soon to find out. The guards were herding us like sheep from one corral to the next.

The steel door opened, and there was a small bench. Above me was no ceiling, and I could see the IDF guards watching me. I sat on the bench. I was tired, so I lay down on the bench and fell asleep. At this point I did not know what had happened to Peter. After what seemed an eternity I was woken up by the blare of the loudspeaker. 'Suheal, wake up. Wake up!'

In a daze and semi-comatose, I stood up. 'Walk to the door.' I did as commanded.

The metal door swished open. There inside was a three-metre-square room with a metal grill on the floor. There was a two-way mirror on the wall, surveillance cameras on the ceiling, and a conveyor belt in one corner.

'Take off your clothes,' said the loudspeaker. I did as commanded and stood in my boxer shorts. 'I said take off *all* your clothes and put them on the conveyor belt.'

I was a bit taken aback. Still in a daze, I was standing on a floor with a metal grill, not knowing what was underneath the grill. Water? Sharks? it was something out of James Bond!

'What is your problem?' I said to the mirror, knowing full well I was being watched. 'Do you all like watching men naked?'

'Take off all your clothes and put them onto the belt now!' came the reply.

I was not ashamed of being naked, but I know for Arabs it can be degrading. After all, in my youth I had been to nudist beaches.

So I laughed again, jeering at the guards. I was not scared, nor was I ashamed. I stood in that room for God knows how long, and then finally my clothes reappeared on the conveyor belt.

'Put your clothes on and go through the door.'

I did as I was commanded. The other steel door opened automatically, and I found myself back into the original room where I had entered from Gaza.

A guard came out and asked me to follow him. At the customs desk were two guards smiling at me. My bag had been turned inside out, and one said in a gruff voice, 'Put your things back in your bag and go to immigration.'

I was livid. As I put my belongings back into my bag, Peter appeared. 'What happened? It's been two hours. They told me to go through immigration, but I told them I would not go anywhere until you came out.'

I looked at Peter and said with a wry smile, 'They were trying to get into my head. Little chance of that.'

Peter and I approached the immigration desk. Peter was allowed straight through, and I was told to wait. So I sat down on the bench and shouted at Peter to wait while I rang the Foreign and Commonwealth Office in Jerusalem.

By this time, I was dying to go to the toilet, so I knocked on the window of the immigration officer, a pretty little Jewish girl, and told her I needed the toilet.

She told me to wait, so I told her I would go and piss in the corner of the waiting room. I turned away and headed off to pee against the wall.

'Stop!' Came a shriek over the loudspeaker. I ignored it and unzipped my trousers. 'OK, OK! Come through,' said the guard.

By this time I had had enough of the IDF's barbaric way of treating people. I walked through the immigration gates into the toilets flanked by two IDF guards. 'You wanna come and hold my dick?' I asked the guards. They looked away in disgust.

On my way back through the immigration counter I came across the colonel who had originally let me through into Gaza. So I asked him what the delay was. He was quite apologetic and said it was routine. 'What,' I replied, 'Routine harassment of anyone with an Arabic name?'

Eventually, after another hour I was allowed into Israel. Peter and I headed to Jerusalem with the taxi that had been arranged for us by Yacoob.

The following day, after a good meal and a good night's rest in Jerusalem, Peter and I headed for the Tel Aviv airport. As we approached the airport we were stopped at the IDF checkpoint; they looked at our passports.

'Get out of the car,' they ordered us both. We were led into a security room with our bags and through an X-ray scanner. Then we were asked some banal questions and told to go on our way to the terminal.

At the check-in desk my passport was scrutinized and my bag turned upside down. As my things fell onto the counter, my Dictaphone came into view. Horrified, the girl at the security desk rang someone. Within minutes I was surrounded by IDF guards.

'Come this way, sir,' one of them ordered me. I was led off into a room, stripped, searched, and then asked to sit at a table. Opposite me stood an IDF guard. He was about 6'4" tall and built like a thug, and as he looked at me he crunched his knuckles into his palm. All I could do was laugh. The whole incident had been blown out of proportion, and here some guard was trying to intimidate me.

In walked a bespectacled, well-dressed man in his thirties. He introduced himself as an officer from Mossad.

'Why were you trying to tape us, Suheal?'

I burst out laughing. 'What was I going to achieve by taping you lot? It was your guard that upturned my bag. The Dictaphone dropped out and hit the "on" button. Listen to what's on the tape.'

The huge guard behind the Mossad officer cracked his knuckles again. I smiled and winked at him, which made him go red in the face.

'We know who you are, where you live, and that your cat is called Max.'

I replied, 'Am I supposed to get scared? I haven't done anything wrong, just helped a few Gazans you blew up.'

'You will stay here until the time for boarding, and then you will be escorted to the plane.'

When the time for boarding arrived, I had two armed guards either side of me, one carrying my bag. 'I love having a valet to carry my things,' I said, smiling. The guards were not amused. I was using some of my own psychology on them.

Once on the plane, I reflected at what had happened over the last few days. The Israelis by nature were paranoid. They used intimidation tactics trying to dissuade foreigners from coming back to their country. What it actually did for me was to strengthen my resolve. I had not been frightened. I was not in the wrong, but I was at the whim of the IDF and Mossad. I knew my e-mails were being monitored and my phone calls tapped back in the United Kingdom.

But I was not a terrorist; I was a humanitarian and would continue with my quest. I could not wait to get back to Gaza again and face the gauntlet once more!

Once, I decided to return to Gaza through Egypt, as I had a meeting in Cairo. Logically, I thought it would be easier to travel up to Rafah and across the border. The WHO had given me a zero-dollar contract, meaning I was officially a member of the WHO, and they would assist in the paperwork to get permission for me to cross at Rafah.

All was in order when I arrived at the border, but the guards sent me away, saying my name was not on a list for passage into Gaza. I was confused and rang the WHO. They told me all was in order. So, I returned the next day and explained my position to the border guards. Reluctantly, they let me into the immigration hall. There I sat for four hours whilst all the rest of the people were processed. Finally, a rude guard told me to come to the desk for questioning. The guards spoke to me in Arabic, but I pretended I did not understand, even though I have a good grasp of the language. Thinking I couldn't understand, they started talking amongst themselves, saying, 'Why should a British Asian be allowed into Gaza to help the people? Let's make his life difficult so he will not come back!'

I just smiled and waited. I was not going to get angry, and I had a good book. I was happy to read whilst I waited. Finally, the officer came up and said that all was in order and that I had to pay a visa fee for entry. When I reached Gaza, a car was waiting to whisk me away to Gaza City and my apartment. Why the Egyptians had been so difficult I do not know. Why they tried to intimidate me I do not know. This experience reinforced my awareness that it's the Israelis who control the borders into Gaza. The Egyptians do what their master tells them.

One of the things I did not understand was how the families and relatives of the Gazan officials had easy access into and out of Gaza whereas the poor, unconnected people struggled to obtain permits to travel outside of Gaza.

Some patients sought medical treatment in Egypt or Israel for their problems, and many told me they had to pay large bribes to the Gazan officials to obtain permits! Some of these patients had been given suboptimal treatment, and I had to re-operate on many of them to fix their original problem.

7

Life in the Gaza Strip

Before I went to Gaza, I thought I would find a cohesive group of people who were deeply religious, strong, and courageous to the core. I was not far wrong. There was a religious fervour to Gaza. In my fourth month in the Gaza Strip, a decree was issued from the administration that women were no longer allowed to smoke *shisha* in public. I felt disappointed, as now I could not enjoy the company of my friend and secretary R at a shisha café. Although a large percentage of women were allowed to enter university and seek higher qualifications, there was still a medieval feel to Gaza. Paradoxically, medieval Islam was an all-encompassing faith allowing different cultures and creeds to live together in harmony. I have seen similar cultural beliefs in rural parts of India: women are covered in burqas, not allowed to drive, and never seen in public. This show of faith is more a cultural than a religious edict.

Moreover, Gaza was a tribal society. Certain families controlled areas, running the schools, hospitals, and other administrative agencies. Everyone knew everyone else. I dubbed the Gazans the Afghans of the Middle East because they were equally ferocious warriors who were fearless, sure they had God on their side, but were backwards in some of their attitudes towards women and progress.

Gaza City was like any other Mediterranean city I had visited (Figures 33, 34, and 35).

**View from my hotel room in Gaza City
showing the beach and dock area**

**View from my fourth-floor office in
Gaza City showing the skyline**

**View from my fourth-floor office showing
the central business district of Gaza City**

The city was full of whitewashed buildings with flat roofs where people gathered in the cool of the evening to watch the sunset and the view. There were apartment blocks, shopping malls, restaurants, coffee shops, and other great places to mill about and talk. The main thoroughfare through Gaza City was called Omar Mukhtar Street, after the infamous Libyan freedom fighter. In 1931, the Italians had captured an injured Omar. After a three-day trial, the Italians found him guilty and publically hanged him at his age of seventy. Omar obviously became an instant martyr and hero amongst the Arab world.

Mukhtar Street ran from Palestine Square to the port of Gaza, separating the old city's al Daraj and Zaytoun quarters. Mukhtar Street was very modern, and most of the good hotels and restaurants were situated on this road. There were many malls for shopping, hundreds of street vendors, and a constant mill of people.

Many of my friends and colleagues would meet in one of these coffee shops selling wonderful espressos and divine cakes. Most of the financial hub lay in this city, and northerners looked down on their southern cousins as if they were country bumpkins.

Travelling from Gaza City in the north, where I had rented an apartment, to Khan Yunis in the south, where I worked at Nasser Hospital, was like travelling back in time.

Khan Yunis was an agrarian society. Many of the families had lived there for generations, and everyone knew each other.

In the evening I would join friends for dinner on the beachfront, where a fish meal was in order. The food was amazing! The Gazans loved their chilies, and the famous Gazan paste, a red concoction of chilies and oil, soon became a favourite of mine.

The Gazans are sociable people and love having dinners and drinking coffee. I enjoyed the way we would sit at a table with the food in the centre. Everyone ate out of this central plate of rice and lamb or *makloobah,* a favourite of Gazans. I always tried to tunnel my way across the plate, to the amusement of my guests. Some of the best food I have ever eaten was in Gaza. The locals referred to this tasty food as *'barraka'* or a blessing from God.

One evening I arrived at the home of a Palestinian aid worker, K, who had invited me to his house. K had done his postgraduate studies in Germany and spoke fluent German. We all sat down for dinner with his wife and children. This surprised me, as normally, a Palestinian would not have a guest eat with his wife unless he was a relative. I think because K had spent most of his formative years in Europe, he was a bit more European than Gazan. K had two children, a boy aged six and girl aged eight. We all talked and discussed life over dinner. They all wished they could go on holiday to Cyprus again, enjoy the simple things in life, and be able to plan for the future. This uncertainty was difficult to handle.

There was chicken on the menu, a favourite of mine. However, his two children did not eat any chicken. So I asked why not. Reluctantly, K told me he had just killed the chicken that morning and it used to be the children's pet! I struggled to eat any more. That was what Gazans were like. They would give you their shirt from their backs if need be!

When I first arrived in Gaza, I expected a shortage of food and water due to the blockade, but this was relatively unfounded. The markets were bustling with fresh produce and spices, some brought through the tunnels and some carried legitimately through the border crossings or grown locally (Figures 36, 37, and 38).

Market in Gaza City

Delivering fruit to a Gaza market stall

Spice shop in a Gaza City open-air market

Transport of goods in Gaza City

Towards the north of the Gaza Strip, I discovered a restaurant and hotel overlooking the Mediterranean Sea called The Madhaf, or Museum. The place was built on an archaeological site, and the artefacts were displayed in the foyer. There were Greek and Roman antiquities, making one realize how many civilizations have lived in and ruled Gaza. The food and service were as excellent as at any five-star hotel in London. I spent many an evening there having dinner with friends, looking out at the beautiful beach and sea.

On another occasion, I was invited to the French consulate, which was holding an exhibition of paintings from local artists (Figure 40). There I met many artists, and a particular one, Ihad Sabbah (Figure 41), inspired me with his paintings and talk. I really enjoyed this bohemian evening, and it was pleasing to see how the Palestinians valued art and literature

(Figure 42). Simple things like this kept me sane and helped me enjoy my stay in Gaza.

French consulate in Gaza City

Author (on left) with artist Ihab Sabbah

One evening, after work, I was invited to a sports centre situated in the north of the Gaza Strip. The local doctors had arranged an evening for me there. After an hour with a personal trainer who nearly killed me, I went for a swim in the pool followed by a massage insisted on by my medic friends. I did not try the sauna, as I hate such things! We sat and enjoyed some kebabs, and life was back to normal for me. There are many places to see and get entertained in Gaza.

On Friday, my day off, I would head to the beach with my lacrosse sticks. There I would meet up with regular enthusiasts and would have a game of lacrosse on the beach. I was impressed at how quickly the children caught onto the game. Soon they were passing and catching the ball in their sticks like professionals! (Figures 43a and 43b)

Playing lacrosse with the children of Gaza on the beach

I really enjoyed my free time with these children. Teaching them and seeing how keen they were to learn a new sport was a joy. My next plan was to set up a windsurfing school, as the waves and the wind were ideal for such a sport.

It was an honour as an *ajnabee* (foreigner) to be invited to dinner with officials from the visiting Islamic Development Bank (IDB) based in Saudi Arabia and high-ranking Hamas politicians. The Gazans had adopted me as their own, as I had shown my commitment to helping them develop and train local surgeons, thereby improving the local health infrastructure.

The delegation from the IDB was a Syrian living in New York, a Sudanese man based in Khartoum, and an Arab from Saudi Arabia. After the initial introductions, the three were interested to hear from me what kind of development was needed for Gaza.

The reception for the IDB was held on the beach under cover of a tarpaulin. We ate some good Gazan food out of plastic trays, sitting on plastic chairs under the dark evening sky. I was surprised not to be eating in one of the Gazan five-star hotels, such as the Madhaf.

During the conversation, I put forward a suggestion that instead of building a diesel-run power station in Gaza as planned, they should invest in solar and wind power. This was ecologically sound and would stop the reliance on the Israelis for the supply of diesel. Israel can and has stopped the supply of oil, bringing Gaza to a halt. Of course, none of my suggestions were taken, as the IDB had a vested interest in selling their oil and products to Gaza.

In May 2010, a Turkish ship carrying aid and medical equipment to Gaza was attacked by the Israelis in international waters, killing some of the relief workers on board. The Gaza Strip came to a standstill. Three days of mourning for the victims was decreed by Hamas, and most Gazans came out on the streets in protest rallies and to show support for the innocent victims of the attack by the IDF (Figures 44 and 45).

Demonstration in Gaza following attack by Israel on Turkish relief vessel, the *Marmara*, in May 2010

**Meeting the Turkish delegation in Gaza
after the attack on their ship by Israel**

There was a sense of seriousness in the air as well as a party atmosphere. The whole population of the Gaza Strip had made their way to the ports in large crowds, showing their support and gratitude to the ill-fated Turkish ship.

Whilst in Gaza, I was told many stories of what life had been like when the Israelis occupied Gaza with the IDF and Jewish settlers. The settlers were mainly concentrated in the middle section of Gaza, the most fertile area. When a settler wanted to go into Israel, the IDF would put up roadblocks so the settlers could leave Gaza unmolested. This would mean effectively splitting Gaza into three sections with two main roadblocks, one in the north and the other in the south. The traffic would be stopped, so if you were travelling from the south to Gaza City, you might get stuck in the middle section. One was not allowed to get out of the vehicle, so people roasted in their cars in the sun. On occasions, the roadblocks would be up for a day or so with no explanation from the IDF soldiers. People caught in the middle sections had to stay in their cars until the IDF decided to re-open the main road.

Many of the Gazans under the Israeli occupation had jobs in Israel. This was a form of cheap labour for the Israelis but a lifeline to many Gazan families, who could earn a bit of money for the upkeep of their families. On a daily basis, starting at four in the morning Gazans would stand in a line at the Erez border, waiting to cross into Israel. There were no jobs in the strip because the industry and factories had been destroyed by Israel. The Israelis had a captive and ready supply of labour. Most had no alternative. If a Gazan committed any misdemeanour, he would not be allowed access to Israel and effectively his family would be worse off.

So for this reason the Gazans would stand in line for hours on end waiting for the IDF to open the crossing at Erez. On occasions, for the soldiers' amusement, the Gazans would be asked to stand on one leg or to keep their right arm raised for no apparent reason. Again, humiliation was a good psychological tactic. Anyone not complying would be led out of line and told they were not to cross that day, losing a day's pay. Many returned after a day's work at one in the morning to get a quick nap before again returning to stand in line at four. It was a hard life but the only one the Gazans knew.

After the Israelis left, Gazan unemployment rocketed, and many families relied on hand-outs from the United Nations High Commissioner for Refugees UNHCR for their families to survive.

Another tale told by a Gazan colleague, M, was as follows. M's father, a teacher, was in his school office one evening, marking the previous week's test papers. The school was empty. M was a twelve year old and a typical boisterous boy who dreamed of travelling and making a living as a lawyer. He had come to school that evening to keep his father company. It was too noisy at home to mark papers, as there was not much room in their three-bedroom apartment for M and his four siblings.

M was in the adjoining classroom playing a game common among Gazan boys: pretending to be a fighter attacking the IDF to end the oppression that most children had known since birth. In his hand he had a metal ruler he was using as his weapon, running up and down the classroom.

With an almighty crash, six IDF soldiers rushed into the classroom, shouting and screaming for M to put down his 'weapon' and to put his hands up. M stood like a statue, dropping his ruler and nearly emptying his bladder in the process.

Hearing all the commotion, M's father entered the room only to be jumped on by two soldiers and held on the ground. 'What is going on? Why have you entered my school? What have we done?'

'Sir, please, there is someone in the school with a weapon, either a gun or a knife. Our guards in the watch tower opposite have witnessed someone in this school with a weapon, and we need to investigate.'

'But the only two in the school are my son and I. There is no one else in the school to my knowledge,' retorted M's father.

'We need to find this sniper, sir. We are not leaving until we do.'

A voice came over on the radio; it was the guard from the watch tower. 'That is the man you are looking for. He had a weapon in his right hand, and it was glistening in the sunlight.'

The soldiers by this stage had surrounded M. At his feet lay a metal ruler.

'But I was just playing,' said M. 'I was holding a ruler, not a gun.'

'Is this the suspect?' asked the soldier into his radio.

'Yes,' crackled the reply from the guards.

'The boy had a ruler in his hand,' said the soldier as he picked it up.

'That's the weapon,' replied the guard. The ruler glistened in the sun through the window.

'It's a *ruler*,' retorted the soldier.

The soldier picked up M by the scruff of his neck and led him out of the door. 'We are taking him for questioning,' he told his father and led M off.

That was the kind of insane paranoia the Gazans had to deal with on a daily basis. IDF soldiers who were no more than boys and on many occasions civilians had been shot for no fault of their own, simply for being in the wrong place at the wrong time.

***

At four in the morning in April of 2004, there was a loud knock on the door of M's house. 'Open up, open up!'

X, a Palestinian father living in Rafah, raced to the door to be confronted by six heavily armed IDF soldiers. 'We need you all to come and help on the road!'

'What?' asked M's father.

'Bring your sons and follow us,' shouted the IDF officer.

Without any further questions, X gathered up his four sons, aged between ten and seventeen years old, and followed the soldiers.

The day before, in Rafah, there had been a bomb attack on an IDF checkpoint. No one had been killed, but there was a lot of wreckage and carnage on the road. The IDF would always get the local people up out of their beds at an ungodly hour for them to clean up the mess. This was a regular occurrence when the Israelis occupied Gaza Strip.

***

It was a pleasant, sunny day in June 2010, and I was standing on the balcony of my office on the fourth floor of the Bursh al Arab building in downtown Gaza City. I smoked a cigarette and looked down at the street bustling with people and cars. The beach was four hundred metres away to my left and the centre of Gaza City to my right.

Without any warning there was a huge explosion three blocks away towards the city centre. A car had been hit by a rocket. Instead of running away, hundreds of people ran towards the scene of the burning car, shouting and screaming. The normal human reaction to a bombing is to run away from such devastation, but the Gazans do not have this response. The attack had been carried out by an Israeli drone. Often, after a first bomb the Israelis would send another rocket killing other bystanders and helpers at such a scene. Thank God, this time it was just the one rocket.

Two brothers had been inside the car. They were members of the Salafis, a puritanical religious group based in southern Gaza. The Salafis are rivals to Hamas, the ruling political party in Gaza.

After the car had been doused with water, the charred bodies remained sitting upright in the car. Many Gazans were wailing and pointing to the sky, shouting profanities at the Israelis.

Within thirty minutes the car had been cleared off the street, leaving a charred patch of road. There had been no other causalities, and life in Gaza City carried on.

Who had directed the drone to the car? How did the Israelis know when and where to hit the car? Why had the car been hit on that day?

These questions were answered by my friend, a journalist, whom I met later in a coffee shop; he will remain unnamed. The Palestinians and the Israelis were in collaboration when it came to such assassinations. A spotter on the ground would mark the victim's car with a laser pen, and this would help guide the Israelis to their intended target.

Gaza has seen many different religions and customs over the ages. Within Gaza, there are about two thousand Greek Orthodox Christians who have been living in Gaza since well before the time of the Muslims. One of the churches in Gaza has been converted into a mosque, and one can still see the font and cathedral-like windows in the building still standing today. The Christian population remains in Gaza, having no other place to go, and as a community, they do not suffer racism as in other Middle East countries from the local Muslim population. The Gazans are tolerant, as long as customs do not spill over into the community. One does not see any bars where the Christians and, for that matter, Muslims would go and drink. Gaza on the surface looks plain and simple – Zionists versus Muslims – but living in Gaza gives one a different perspective of the struggle.

8
Health System and Education

The Gaza Strip has three main teaching hospitals: Al Shifa in Gaza City, Nasser Hospital in Khan Yunis, and the European Gaza Hospital (EGH) in the South. Other hospitals have autonomy but are smaller and dotted around the strip (Figure 46).

Hospitals in the Gaza Strip

Amongst the doctors there was a heterogeneity of levels and standards due to the fact that many had been taught medicine in a foreign language (usually Russian or Turkish), as at their time of study there was no medical school in the Gaza Strip. Some of the doctors had been on scholarships, with their course fees paid by sponsors. Unfortunately, these doctors were few and far between.

More funding and thought should be given to local sustainability. One should be thinking of training the trainers, to improve medical practices locally. More funded scholarships and exchange programmes should be given to Gazan doctors. Following my return from my first visit to Gaza, I published a paper in the *Journal of Perioperative Practice* (Oct. 2010, Vol. 20, 368–371, for any of those interested). The paper highlighted the orthopaedic needs for the Gaza Strip. The paper mainly focused on improving local infrastructure and training of doctors and allied health care professionals to help improve the quality of health care provision.

Many patients preferred to go to Egypt or Israel for complex medical treatment. The MoH would get many letters a month from locals requesting permission for treatment abroad. The funding for the treatment would come from the MoH, which ultimately would be paid by the West Bank Administration. There was no nuclear medicine or radiotherapy suite in the Gaza Strip. This was mainly due to the paranoia of the Israelis, who thought the radio isotopes needed to run these medical machines may lead to a nuclear bomb!

Many experienced Gazan doctors collected a salary from the Fateh regime in the West Bank for staying at home rather than working, so as not to help the Hamas administration. One evening in November 2010, I met a group of such 'unemployed' doctors, all very amicable, eloquent, and experienced doctors and surgeons. As we sat together, the conversation inevitably turned towards politics. All present were happy and pleased I had returned to Gaza to teach and train the local surgeons. Their only grudge was the fact that the Hamas government insisted that they remain at home and not work as their salary was being paid by the West Bank, controlled by the Fatah regime. It was very frustrating for some of these doctors, but what could they do? In my opinion, politics should not interfere with practicing as a doctor. This put me in some difficulties, but as I reiterated to all and everyone in the room, I was in Gaza on a humanitarian mission and not here to take sides in a long and hard-fought political struggle between Hamas and Fateh. It must have been difficult both mentally and financially for these professionals; these doctors were not allowed to carry on with their private practice, which was an added monthly income. I was never told about this group of doctors on my first visit to Gaza. If it had not been for one of my colleague in Khan Yunis, I may never have known about the real situation.

In July 2010, the Minister of Health invited me into his office. With the customary salutations, tea was served. The reason for the meeting was that the minister had been impressed with the way I had changed some of the working practices in Nasser Hospital's orthopaedic department. He asked if I would be interested in taking over as head of the department, since the current head would be moving to Al Shifa Hospital in Gaza City. I would also work one day a week at the European Gaza Hospital (EGH).

Having worked in Gaza for three months as a visiting professor, I was pleased to see that my actions and intentions had been noted by the powers that be. The brother of the minister of health was an orthopaedic surgeon and had helped in instigating and initiating some of the changes on my suggestion such as morning trauma meetings, preop anaesthetic clins and so on.

A Gaza Orthopaedic Association was formed on my suggestion, when I was Head of Orthopaedics at Nasser Hospital, and we met on a monthly basis to discuss clinical cases and socialise. I wished that eventually each hospital would host a monthly meeting. This would spread knowledge and cohesiveness amongst the orthopaedic surgeons. With the help of the local surgeons, we devised an educational programme for the local trainees consisting of lectures and case discussions. This programme was to help the local surgeons pass their Arab Board Examinations before full registration was granted, allowing them to practice as independent surgeons. This initiative was also to help build camaraderie and team spirit amongst the residents.

In Gaza, there were established public hospitals run by the MoH and private hospitals run by consortiums or individuals, much the same as we see in the West. Having visited these private hospitals, I knew that their facilities and available kit were far superior to those in the public hospitals. I was very impressed by the look and professionalism of the staff at these institutions, which could have easily been state-of-the-art hospitals in Jordan or Tel Aviv.

Palestinians value education and knowledge above everything else. At the Islamic University of Gaza 55 per cent of the students were women, a refreshing statistic as one views the Islamic world as oppressive to its women. In fact this oppression is mainly perpetuated by the Taliban in Afghanistan.

This political struggle was also reflected in the medical schools in Gaza. I was under the impression there was only one medical school in Gaza based at the Islamic University of Gaza (IUG).

On my first visit to Gaza, we were shown round the Medical School at IUG. The school had been established in 2006 and was well equipped with a computer laboratory, a virtual anatomy lab, and a very bright young bunch of students eager to learn (Figure 47).

Islamic University of Gaza (IUG) medical school

After giving the medical students a talk on orthopaedics, I was approached by some students asking why I had come to Gaza. I told them about the humanitarian mission and MiST. They just laughed and told me I was there to learn from the brilliant Gaza surgeons. I smiled and agreed with them.

Prior to this medical school, many doctors had been taught abroad in a myriad of languages. There clinical knowledge was heterogeneous, to say the least.

In fact, there were two medical schools in Gaza. Al Azhar University in Gaza City had a medical school established in 2001. I visited that school on my return to Gaza and gave some lectures to the students there. I asked why I had not been shown around on my first visit. The staff at the university explained they were Fateh sympathizers, and thus the Hamas administration supported IUG, so foreign doctors were exclusively shown around that former university. This division was not for me to get involved in; I was there after all to treat and teach anyone, irrespective of colour, creed, or political affiliations. Some of the local surgeons were paid by the university to lecture and teach. Their students and their clinical studies were randomly allocated to various hospitals dotted around the Gaza Strip.

Medical kit and equipment for operations were always scarce, and once, in my monthly meeting with health officials, I had raised the point. If you can bring anything through the tunnels, surely you can bring surgical kit? This remark was not well received. I had been waiting for my $350 000 worth of kit to arrive from Egypt. But there were delays, and the paperwork was taking a long time.

The Gazan government receives monies from aid agencies, from the West Bank Administration, and from generous donations from around the world. One of my sources told me about an aid agency that pays the MoH $10 000 a month to stay in Gaza. This same agency probably makes a million dollars a month in donations. This agency had funded sixteen physiotherapists to work in Gaza, but they were treating non-unions and mal-unions of bones by exercise and not the operative intervention that was needed for these patients!

Where is all the money going? It is not for me to ask ...

An aid agency in Manchester had agreed to send some of the MiST Foundation medical kit stored in their warehouse in the United Kingdom on their next convoy trip to Gaza. I was pleasantly surprised. So when the convoy arrived a few months later, there was a great party atmosphere in Gaza City. My kit was handed over with lots of photos and hugs from the UK convoy (Figure 48).

**Convoy arrives at Al Shifa hospital with
medical supplies from the UK**

When I opened the kit, all the metal boxes were empty! I was surprised and a bit taken aback to learn that this was an empty photo opportunity. It turned out to be a way for an aid agency to portray itself as doing some good in sending medical equipment to Gaza, so they could raise more donations for the cause.

One day, I was taken to a warehouse acting as a medical equipment store. Most of the kit had been donated from around the world, but a lot of the equipment was obsolete and useless. A Middle East country had sent one million dollars-worth of vaccines, but their shipment was out of date and useless. One of the managers of the warehouse told me that Gaza had become the dumping ground for medical equipment. As the Gazans were polite and could not refuse donations, the Gaza Strip had the biggest warehouse of useless, outdated kit. Surely it had been a great photo opportunity for certain aid agencies and governments when the donations were originally made.

9

The Working Week

Gaza had a six-day working week, with Fridays as a day off. On each working day, a taxi or ambulance would pick me up from my apartment at 7.30 a.m. in Gaza City and drive along the coast road to Khan Yunis and Nasser Hospital. I always insisted in going and coming back this way. The road was not as good as the only main north-south road in Gaza, but I could look out over the Mediterranean on my journey to and from work. Watching the waves crash along the shore was a soothing start to the day (Figure 49).

Coast road heading back from Khan Yunis to Gaza City; Mediterranean shown on left.

The fishermen would be out along the seashore on their flat-top rafts and long poles steering their craft. Children would be on the road going to school. Because there were so many children and not enough schools, there would be three shifts at school: morning, afternoon, and evening classes (Figures 50, 51, and 52).

Children leaving school in Khan Yunis

Tank tracks from an Israeli tank made into a sandpit for the children to play

School is out in Khan Yunis

It was July 2010, and I had taken up my appointment as head of orthopaedics at Nasser Hospital. The staff had been very accommodating and welcomed the changes I had introduced into their working practices.

Of the medical staff there were three trainees, five medical officers/house officers, and three associate specialists (who were between trainees and consultants in the hospital hierarchy). AS was a non-training post and these three doctors could operate independently of the consultants. Out of courtesy, the three AS's would ask my permission to do a procedure and then slot the patient in their next available operation list.

On my first visit to Gaza, I had trained the nursing staff in theatre on the different types of kit needed to apply a ring fixator. On my arrival, the staff had neatly put all the different components of the kit into metal trays, which could be autoclaved, and everything had been labelled and catalogued. I was deeply impressed at the nursing staff's professionalism.

We now had a trauma meeting every morning starting at eight, where we discussed the previous night's admissions and the cases that had been booked for theatre that day. This would be followed by a ward round at eight thirty and then either theatres or outpatient clinics starting at nine.

Once a week, the residents would present a thirty-minute talk on an orthopaedic topic and teach their peers. This way they kept up with the literature and academic activities.

The outpatient clinic was a melee, with patients trying to get to the front of the queue, waving their X-rays above their heads! There was a room with a long desk where four doctors sat facing the door waiting for patients. The day usually started as a scrum with many patients wishing to be seen first and no concept of queuing. After two weeks of such mayhem, I told the director of the hospital about the situation. He installed a security guard at the door, who would vet the patients and send them into the room one by one. A bit of order was created out of chaos!

In this room, I kept an eye on the juniors and was there for any advice or concerns the doctors had. The system worked quite well, and the doctors knew I was approachable for any kind of problem. I was there also to follow up with the patients on whom the MiST Foundation had operated.

In a small side room, a nurse would sit. Here the dressings and wounds were examined, cleaned, and re-dressed. Any small practical procedures were carried out in this room under a local anaesthetic, if any was available!

Lunch was served in the cafeteria, paid for by the hospital administration. So the place was always full. It was a good place to meet other doctors and allied health care professionals, and a bit of banter was always exchanged.

Once a week, some of the senior doctors would go to their 'rooms' in the evenings for their private practice. This was a way of making some extra money, a practice I have seen in many countries around the world. I had no qualms about these doctors finding a way of increasing their monthly salary.

Having visited a private hospital in Gaza, I knew that the facilities and kit there were far superior to the public hospitals. This is what one sees in other countries as well.

The three theatres in Nasser Hospital were clean but rudimentary. Off to the side was a recovery room where patients waited both before and after operative procedures. Moreover, most patients were wheeled into the corridor awaiting their turn for their procedure. Invariably, the X-ray machine would not work, and so I did not rely on intraoperative X-rays for doing my operations.

The anaesthetists were very experienced, and most of their work was done by giving local blocks to patients without specialized ultrasound machines as in the West. This saved a lot of time, and all the blocks worked. The patient would be awake during the operation but feel no pain as the procedure progressed. I was really impressed by the professionalism and expertise of these anaesthetists. They never once refused to work and often stayed behind so I could finish a complex operation; this was a pleasant change to what we find in the West.

Once a week I would spend a day at the European Gaza Hospital in Rafah, in the southern Gaza Strip, starting with an eight o'clock trauma meeting with all the staff. EGH had been funded and founded by the European Union in the early 1990s. It was the newest hospital and had recently been linked to the Islamic University of Gaza for the training of their medical students.

Working with the staff was a joy. They had never seen ring fixators applied to limbs but soon were into the swing of things. The head of department was a well-read, deeply religious man. He was about five years older than me and spoke with a soft voice and humility. In theatre, he became a psychopath! It has always amused me how people cope under stress. Some become introverted; others rant and rave.

In the evenings, I would run an outpatient clinic from six to eight from my hotel reception area. The owner of the hotel was happy to oblige and would give me a table and a quiet corner of the foyer where I could see patients in private. Patients would turn up for consultation and advice. After the first two months of doing this free clinic, I realized that most of the patients were relatives or friends from the Islamic University or Hamas party, and most were from well-to-do families. I thus started to charge a hundred shekels per consultation. The numbers of patients dropped off dramatically except for the poor! They continued to come even though they had to pay. The rich and well-connected never came again. On occasions, once the consultation was over and I could see that the patients and relatives were in a desperate financial situation, I would return them their hundred shekels and give them some extra from the funds I had collected in the United Kingdom for such Gazan people (Figure 53).

**Being awarded a memento by Palestinians
for work in the Gaza Strip**

10
Closing Remarks

The country where one is born shapes one's life. Being born in the Gaza Strip means a life behind walls. There is no end to this conflict in sight in the world's largest open prison, the Gaza Strip.

On the surface, the Gazan conflict looks like Palestinians versus Zionists. But the truth is far from reality. What we see and hear in the media does not truly reflect what is happening or has happened in Palestine for the last sixty years.

The conflict goes much deeper than just opposing religions. It's a power struggle between the state of Israel and its neighbouring countries. Egypt has aided Israel by protecting the southern border of Gaza, and Jordan protects the eastern border of Israel.

This alienation from the outside world just breeds contempt and radicalism in the population of Gaza. A vicious cycle is perpetuated, with both sides claiming victories, bullying their populations, and keeping them under wraps. After all, money is power, and power is control.

I personally do not foresee an end to this apartheid in my lifetime. This conflict will add fuel to other radical groups around the world, constituting an excuse to kill more innocent people.

Citizens of the World wake up and unite against oppression and radicalism. We want a safe, prosperous world for the next generation.

About the Author

Suheal Ali Khan is a son of an immigrant family who moved from India to the United Kingdom in the 1960s. Born and bred in Manchester, Suheal went to medical school in Sheffield. Following qualification in 1987, Suheal progressed in his medical career and was appointed as a consultant orthopaedic surgeon in 1999.

In 2003, Suheal moved to a university teaching hospital in Manchester, where he ran the limb reconstruction unit specializing in the Ilizarov technique and correction of limb deformity. He is the founder and director of the MiST Foundation (www.mistngo.co.uk). The foundation established in 2005 in the aftermath of the South East Asian earthquake, and many MiST units were sent to Pakistan to help the injured. A limb reconstruction unit was also established in Pakistan during 2006. MiST now works in Cambodia, Nepal, and the West Bank.

Suheal A. Khan

Having left the United Kingdom in 2010, Suheal now lives in the Far East as a visiting professor of orthopaedics and continues with his humanitarian work, including teaching and training of surgeons in developing countries.

The Cover Painting

The painting is by the author depicting the destruction after the IDF bombing of Gaza and is called, **Nowhere to Run**. It shows the Gaza Strip from the sea through a pair of binoculars; the tunnels act as a life line for the Gazan people to continue existing. Otherwise, starvation would be rife.

Appendix 1

RING FIXATORS AND ILIZAROV TECHNIQUE

Gavril A Ilizarov was born in Byelorussia in the former Soviet Union in 1921. Born of illiterate parents, he did not start his formal education until the age of 11. He graduated at the age of 22 in 1943 from medical school. After qualifying he was sent to Kurgan, a small industrial town, in Western Siberia. Ilizarov was the only physician for hundreds of miles and dealt with anything from obstetrics and gynaecology to orthopaedics, with little in the way of medicines or supplies.

Although he did not qualify as a surgeon, he was confronted regularly with a wide variety of orthopaedic problems. A combination of bone deformities, war trauma and industrial accidents forced Ilizarov to use his ingenuity. Through trial and error using handmade equipment he designed his revolutionary **circular external fixator** to treat fractures, deformities and bone defects.

Ilizarov, by serendipity, found that through the use of his ring fixator he could successfully lengthen a limb at a rate of 1mm per day; tension osteogenesis, a term he coined, as is now known as the ***Ilizarov Method***.

This technique has revolutionised Orthopaedics and we can now treat with relative success congenital and acquired limb deformities such as limb length discrepancies, the latter usually through trauma.

Ilizarov continued to work in relative obscurity until 1967 when he successfully treated an infected non-union of the tibia in the Olympic high jumper champion Valery Brumel, a National hero, Ilizarov's technique became famous in Russia.

Ilizarov in 1979, also successfully treated the Italian explorer; Carlo Mauri's infected non-union of his tibia. Carlo already had had eighteen unsuccessful operations to treat his infected tibia.

An Italian doctor Prof Bianchi-Maiocchi, friends of Carlo Mauri, introduced the Ilizarov technique to the West in 1981.

In 1991, the first Ilizarov frame, 40 years after its invention, was applied on a patient in the UK!

Ilizarov continued his work to develop countless clinical applications of bone and soft tissue regeneration until 1992 when he died at the age of 71.

A new Orthopaedic Specialty had been created, *Limb Reconstruction*.

The Ilizarov apparatus

How can a surgeon treat bone fractures, non-unions and mal-unions?

There are only three things ways a surgeon can treat bone surgically;

i) A device in the middle of the bone, in the marrow cavity, called an Intramedullary Nail,

ii) A device on the surface of the bone called Plates and Screws or

iii) A device used on the outside of the bone called an External Fixator, which can consist of rods or rings.

Depending on the orthopaedic condition being treated and patient factors, a surgeon will chose a particular device depending on his experience and surgical knowledge of the pathology to be treated.

What is an Ilizarov frame or Ring Fixator?

One can think of the Ilizarov or ring fixator as a wheel on a cart; the axle is the ***bone***, the wheel is the ***ring*** of the fixator and the spokes of the wheel are the ***fine wires*** and ***pins*** used to secure the ring to the bone.

The Ilizarov frame or ring fixator thus encircles the limb and is made up from a number of circular metal or carbon fibre rings connected to each other by threaded rods. The frame is secured on the limb with wires and/or half-pins.

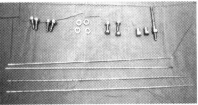

Figure A showing components of Ring Fixator; the metal and carbon fibre half rings with threaded rods.

Figure B showing a selection of fine wires and fixation bolts used to attach the wires to the rings.

Although this external scaffold looks bulky and medieval it provides excellent stability for the injured limb. The ring fixator is highly versatile and robust and the patient can immediately weight bear following the procedure. The threaded rods between the rings can be lengthened or shortened by turning nuts according to the need of the condition.

With the newer designs of ring fixators such as the **hexapod**, the deformity correction is now calculated by a computer and a prescription chart made for the patients, telling them when to adjust each of the struts, by how much on each day of the treatment regime.

This advance has helped both the surgeon and the patient in helping correct deformities; the older method was successful but very time consuming and cumbersome.

Fig C. The Hexapod Ring Fixator shown on left and the Classic Ilizarov frame shown on right; note the struts or threaded rods on Ilizarov are placed vertically whereas in the hexapod the struts are slanted. The hexapod has a greater degree of freedom in deformity correction and thus one does not have to reassemble the frame as in the classic Ilizarov frame which only has 2 degrees of freedom at any given time.

The advantage of ring fixator's use in developing countries is cost! Once the rings are removed from a patient successfully treated, all the components (apart from the wires used to secure the rings to the bone) are sterilized and used again on another patient. This can dramatically reduce the cost, as there are no implants involved which can only be used once and remain in the body of the patient.

Moreover, teaching the Ilizarov methods with the use of computers and IT has dramatically reduced the learning curve in acquiring expertise for use of ring fixators. For instance, once I have taught a surgeon the application of a ring fixator on a limb, using the safe anatomical corridors of wire placement, I can be in another country, receive a post-operative X-ray via email and correct the deformity from afar through the use of a computer programme and the hexapod frame. The prescription for strut adjustment, are duly emailed back to the referring surgeon for use by his patient.

Printed in the United States
By Bookmasters